The Flavours Series

PASTA

ELAINE ELLIOT

Photography by Julian Beveridge

FORMAC PUBLISHING COMPANY LIMITED
HALIFAX 2000

PHOTO CREDITS:
All photographs by Julian Beveridge.

PARTICIPATING ESTABLISHMENTS:
Acton's Grill & Café, Wolfville, NS
Amherst Shore Country Inn, Lorneville, NS
Arbor View Inn, Lunenburg, NS
Billy's Seafood Company, Saint John, NB
Blomidon Inn, Wolfville, NS
Catherine McKinnon's Spot O'Tea
  Restaurant, Stanley Bridge, PEI
Charlotte Lane Café and Crafts,
  Shelburne, NS
Dundee Arms Inn, Charlottetown, PEI
The Dunes, Brackley Beach, PEI
Falcourt Inn, Nictaux, NS
Gabrieau's Bistro, Antigonish, NS

Il Mercato Ristorante, Halifax, NS
The Innlet Café, Mahone Bay, NS
Jubilee Cottage Country Inn, Wallace, NS
The Ledges Inn, Doaktown, NB
Little Shemogue Country Inn, Port Elgin, NB
Liscombe Lodge, Liscomb Mills, NS
Marshlands Inn, Sackville, NB
The Murray Manor Bed and Breakfast,
  Yarmouth, NS
Seasons in Thyme, Summerside, PEI
The Whitman Inn, Kempt, NS
The Windsor House of St. Andrews, St.
  Andrews, NB

This book is dedicated with love to my granddaughter Jessica Elliot of Nova Scotia and grandson Cameron Elliot of New Brunswick.

Formac Publishing Company Limited acknowledges the support of the Cultural Affairs Section, Nova Scotia Department of Tourism and Culture. We acknowledge the financial support of the Government of Canada through the Book Publishing Industry Development Program (BPIDP) for our publishing activities.

Canadian Cataloguing in Publication Data

Elliot, Elaine, 1939–
        Pasta
        (Maritime Flavours)
        Includes index.
        ISBN 0-88780-510-8

1. Cookery (Pasta)   I. Title.   II. Series.
TX809.M17E524 2000   641.8'22   C00-950009-X

Formac Publishing Company Limited
5502 Atlantic Street
Halifax, Nova Scotia
B3H 1G4

Distribution in the United States:
Seven Hills Book Distributors
1531 Tremont Street
Cincinnati, Ohio 45214

Printed in China

CONTENTS

INTRODUCTION

Vermicelli

There is an artist lurking in the soul of every chef! How else could they create such outstanding dishes? In the tenth book of the Flavour Series, chefs from the inns and restaurants of eastern Canada share their pasta masterpieces. Once again, talented photographer Julian Beveridge visited many of the establishments, capturing the dishes as they are served by their creators.

Capellini

Fusilli

water provides the base to which ingredients such as eggs, milk, or vegetable purees of spinach or tomatoes are added. The dough is then pressed through a series of rollers into thin sheets which are cut and formed into various shapes. Fresh pasta is available in most large supermarkets or Italian markets and should be refrigerated in airtight containers for use within 2 – 3 days or frozen for up to one month. Dried pasta, which should be smooth with a translucent creamy to yellow colour, is readily available in dozens of shapes and sizes.

Pasta has been a staple food in many cultures for hundreds of years, however, its prevalence in local cuisine of the northeast is more recent. Good quality pasta is made from gluten-rich semolina, a meal made from coarsely ground durum wheat. Grown in the Mediterranean, Middle East, Russia and the Americas, this grain is ideal, producing a fresh or dried pasta that doesn't absorb a lot of water in the cooking process.

To make pasta, a thick mixture of flour and

Conchiglioni

Tortellini

TO COOK PASTA

The decision of fresh versus dried pasta is usually governed by availability. Fresh pasta cooks more rapidly than dried pasta, in about 3 minutes. Dried pasta requires approximately 10 minutes, depending upon variety, so be sure to follow the instructions on the package. All pasta must be cooked in a large quantity of boiling, salted water, allowing 16 cups of water per half pound. Submerge the pasta and gently stir to keep pieces separated. The term "al dente" refers to the desired texture of the noodle which should feel tender, yet be firm to bite. Pasta should never be soggy and soft. Drain pasta, shaking colander to completely remove water, then serve with your favourite preheated sauce.

How much pasta should you prepare? The amount of fresh or dried pasta you use depends upon personal taste. On average, one pound of dry pasta will serve 6–8.

If the cooked pasta is not being used immediately, drain well and toss gently with 1

Penne

tablespoon of oil, being sure that strands are completely coated. Then either place the pasta in an ovenproof bowl, cover with foil and keep warm at 250°F or refresh reserved pasta by immersing in boiling water to return to serving temperature and again drain thoroughly.

The recipes included in this book call for a variety of pasta shapes, and while many more types are available, a short description follows of those suggested by the chefs. Let your personal preference be your guide and substitute at will!

Ditalini

Rotini

Linguine

Fettuccini

Spaghettini

Capelli d'ancelo

Lasagne

Spaghetti

APPETIZERS

$\mathscr{A}$ppetizers should set the mood for the meal that follows. In this section you will find a variety of enticing "starters," many incorporating seafood.

◄ *Fettuccini with Sea Trout served at Little Shemogue Country Inn*

FETTUCCINI WITH SEA TROUT ON CREAMED SPINACH

LITTLE SHEMOGUE COUNTRY INN, PORT ELGIN, NB

*Always seeking an elegant presentation, owner-chef Petra Sudbrack garnishes the plate
with lemon slices and fresh dill sprigs.*

12 ounces fresh spinach, rinsed and stems removed

1/2 cup heavy cream (35% m.f.)

4 slices bacon, finely diced

1 small onion, finely chopped

1 garlic clove, minced

salt and pepper, to taste

fettuccini to serve 4 as an appetizer

1 pound sea-trout fillets, skinless

1 tablespoon dry white vermouth

pinch pepper

juice from 1/2 fresh lemon

2–3 tablespoons chilled butter

fresh lemon slices and dill sprigs, as garnish

Cook spinach in boiling salted water until wilted, about 2 minutes. Remove from heat and drain completely. Transfer spinach to a blender, add cream and purée.

Fry bacon and onion, until bacon is crisp. Stir in garlic and continue to fry 1 minute. In a small saucepan, combine bacon mixture with spinach mixture and bring to a boil, reduce heat and simmer 3 minutes. Season to taste with salt and pepper, remove from heat and keep warm.

Cook fettuccini in boiling salted water until *al dente*, drain and keep warm.

Preheat oven to 400°F.

While pasta is cooking, divide trout into four servings and place on a lightly greased baking sheet. Sprinkle with vermouth, pepper and lemon juice. Dot with butter and bake until fish is opaque and flakes, approximately 8 minutes.

To serve, divide pasta and spinach sauce between plates and top with trout fillet. Garnish with lemon slices and fresh dill sprigs.

Serves 4.

LISCOMBE LODGE SMOKED SALMON

LISCOMBE LODGE,
LISCOMB MILLS, NS

Nestled on the banks of the Liscomb River, the lodge is famous for salmon dishes. In fact, the most popular entrée features planked salmon cooked over an open fire. This dish calls for traditional "cold" smoked salmon.

3 tablespoons butter

1 tablespoon minced onion

1 tablespoon each diced red and green pepper

1 garlic cloves, minced

1/2 pound smoked salmon, sliced in thin strips

2 tablespoons dry white Vermouth or wine

1/2 cup heavy cream (35% m.f.)

1/4 cup fresh parsley, chopped

capellini or linguine to serve 4, cooked *al dente*

In a skillet, melt butter and sauté onion, peppers, and garlic until soft but not brown. Add salmon, stir and cook for one minute. Stir in Vermouth or wine, increase heat to medium and cook one minute. Stir in cream and half the parsley and simmer a few minutes until sauce is slightly thickened.

Toss drained pasta with sauce and serve garnished with remaining chopped parsley.

Serves 4.

CAPELLINI WITH LEMON AND CAVIAR

JUBILEE COTTAGE COUNTRY INN,
WALLACE, NS

Daphne Dominey of Jubilee Cottage Country Inn states that while any caviar will suffice, presentation is much more outstanding if you use both black and gold caviar.

1 cup heavy cream (35% m.f.)

2 tablespoons vodka

1 teaspoon lemon zest

salt and pepper to taste

1 pound capellini

1/3 cup melted butter

2 tablespoons fresh lemon juice

1 jar caviar (2 ounce)

2 tablespoons finely snipped chives

In a deep skillet, bring cream to boiling point; stir in vodka and lemon zest and season with salt and pepper. Reduce heat and simmer gently, stirring occasionally, for 5 minutes or until sauce has reduced and thickened slightly.

Meanwhile, cook capellini in boiling water until *al dente*.

Place melted butter in a bowl, stir in lemon juice and drained pasta. Pour in cream sauce and toss to coat.

Divide pasta between serving plates; top with a dollop of caviar and garnish with snipped chives.

Serves 8.

CARAMELIZED ONION LINGUINE

THE WINDSOR HOUSE OF ST. ANDREWS, ST. ANDREWS, NB

Chef Patricia Bullock prepares this dish as an appetizer, but notes that it makes a delicious accompaniment to grilled pork chops or roast chicken.

3 pounds white cooking onions

3 tablespoons olive oil

1 teaspoon salt

linguine to serve 4

generous amount of freshly ground black pepper

1 cup freshly grated Parmesan cheese

Peel onions and slice as thinly as possible. Heat oil in a large skillet, add onions and sprinkle with salt. Cook, covered, over medium-low heat, stirring frequently. Once onions are very soft and there is still a little juice in the pan, remove cover and increase heat to medium-high. Stir the onions over the heat until they are caramelized or golden brown.

Cook linguine in boiling salted water until *al dente*.

Using a pair of tongs or a slotted spoon, transfer pasta to onions. Stir and toss with black pepper and Parmesan. If pasta is sticky, add a little of the cooking water. Serve immediately.

Serves 6.

Chef Patricia Bullock's Caramelized Onion Linguine ▶

GABRIEAU'S LINGUINE WITH PROSCIUTTO

GABRIEAU'S BISTRO, ANTIGONISH, NS

At Gabrieau's a variety of grilled vegetables are used depending upon the season and perhaps the whim of chef Mark!

1 tablespoon olive oil

1/2 teaspoon crushed chili peppers

2 teaspoons pine nuts

1/4 pound mixed grilled vegetables

1/4 pound prosciutto, thinly sliced

1 clove garlic, minced

salt and pepper, to taste

1 tablespoon butter

1 tablespoon white wine

8 ounces fresh spinach, rinsed, stems removed and julienned

linguine to serve 4 as an appetizer, cooked *al dente*

2 tablespoons balsamic vinegar

cracked black pepper, as garnish

freshly grated Parmesan cheese, as garnish

parsley sprigs as garnish

Heat olive oil in a large skillet over medium-high. Add crushed chilis and pine nuts and sauté briefly. Add vegetables, prosciutto and garlic. Season with salt and pepper. Stir in butter, wine, spinach, and cooked pasta and sauté only until spinach has wilted. Stir in vinegar and garnish with cracked pepper, Parmesan cheese and fresh parsley.

Serves 4.

A wonderful combination of grilled vegetables in Chef Mark Gabrieau's Linguine with Prosciutto ▶

WILD MUSHROOM RAVIOLI WITH FRESH HERBS AND WHITE TRUFFLE OIL

ARBOR VIEW INN, LUNENBURG, NS

*Pungently aromatic, white truffle oil from Italy's Piedmont region exudes an earthy flavour
and is available in specialty sections of Italian markets and larger grocery stores.*

2 shallots, diced

1 tablespoon olive oil

3 cloves garlic, minced

3 cups mixed mushrooms (shiitake, oyster, cremini, chanterelles)

1/2 cup white wine

salt and pepper, to taste

1/2 cup grated Asiago cheese

1 pound fresh pasta sheets rolled out to 1/8-inch thickness

egg wash (1 teaspoon water whisked with 1 egg white)

3 tablespoons unsalted butter

chopped fresh herbs (parsley, sage, rosemary, thyme, chervil)

white truffle oil

Gently sauté shallots in olive oil until fragrant. Add garlic and sauté a few minutes longer, being careful not to brown the garlic. Clean and coarsely chop the mushrooms. Add mushrooms to pan and continue to sauté until the mushrooms have cooked. Deglaze the pan with wine and continue simmering until all the liquid has evaporated. Season with salt and pepper, fold in cheese and let the mixture cool completely.

Roll out the pasta sheets into 3-inch wide strips. Place 1/2 tablespoon of mushroom mixture onto the pasta, brush sides of pasta with egg wash and cover with another piece of pasta. Using a 2-inch round cutter cut out the stuffed pasta being sure to crimp the edges well. Place ravioli, covered, on a lightly flowered tray and continue until all the pasta and mushroom mixture has been used.

Bring a large saucepan of salted water to the boil, add ravioli allowing 3–4 pieces per person and cook until *al dente*. Gently lift out of water with a slotted spoon and keep warm.

Heat butter over moderate to high heat until foamy. When butter starts to turn brown, add the ravioli, a sprinkle of fresh herbs and season with salt, toss to coat.

Serve with a drizzle of truffle oil and a garnish of fresh herbs.

Serves 4–6.

Chef Daniel Orovec's Wild Mushroom Ravioli ▶

SOUP AND SALAD

*P*asta is a versatile ingredient, ideally suited to hearty soups and sumptuous salads.

◄ *Minestrone as served at Wolfville's Blomidon Inn*

BLOMIDON INN MINESTRONE

BLOMIDON INN, WOLFVILLE, NS

The perfect soup for a chilly winter's day, chef Sean Laceby's minestrone is full of fresh vegetables and small pasta rounds. He suggests cooking the pasta separately, so that it doesn't absorb the liquid from the soup.

1/2 cup olive oil

1 onion, diced

1 cup diced red and green peppers

1 cup carrots, in small dice

2 garlic cloves, minced

1 cup diced celery

1 cup diced zucchini

2 cups vegetable or chicken stock

3 cups stewed tomatoes

4 cups tomato juice

5 dashes each Worcestershire and Tabasco sauces

1 tablespoon basil

1/2 tablespoon dry mustard

3/4 teaspoon oregano

2 bay leaves

salt and pepper, to taste

3/4 cup ditalini, cooked *al dente*

grated Parmesan cheese, for garnish

Heat oil in a large saucepan over medium heat. Stir in onion and sweat it, stirring frequently, for 5 minutes. Add peppers, carrots, garlic, celery and zucchini and continue to cook for 5 minutes. Add stock, stewed tomatoes, tomato juice, Worcestershire sauce, Tabasco sauce, basil, dry mustard, oregano and bay leaves and simmer until vegetables are tender. Remove bay leaves, season with salt and pepper, stir in cooked pasta, serve immediately, garnished with freshly grated Parmesan cheese.

Serves 6–8.

GREEK PASTA SALAD

FALCOURT INN, NICTAUX, NS

To enhance the flavour of this dish, chef Kelvin Boutilier of Falcourt Inn suggests preparing the salad a day before serving, allowing the flavours to blend.

3 cups fusilli

3 vine-ripened tomatoes

1/2 English cucumber

1 red onion

1 cup pitted large black olives, halved

1 cup feta cheese, crumbled

Greek Pasta Salad Dressing, recipe follows

Prepare pasta, drain and set aside.

Chop tomatoes, unpeeled cucumber and onion into a 1/2-inch dice. Combine with pasta in bowl. Stir in olives and cheese. Toss with Greek Pasta Salad Dressing to coat and refrigerate, covered 12–24 hours. Cover and refrigerate remaining salad dressing up to 5 days.

Serves 4–6.

Greek Pasta Salad Dressing

2 tablespoons white vinegar

2 tablespoons balsamic vinegar

2 tablespoons cider vinegar

1 tablespoon white wine

2 tablespoons sugar

2–3 cloves garlic, crushed

1 tablespoon basil

1/2 tablespoon oregano

1 cup extra virgin olive oil

Whisk together the vinegars, wine, sugar, garlic, and herbs in a bowl. Refrigerate 1/2 hour. Slowly pour olive oil in a steady stream into vinegar mixture while whisking vigorously. Yields 1 1/2 cups.

DILLED SHRIMP AND PASTA SALAD

ACTON'S GRILL AND CAFÉ,
WOLFVILLE, NS

The dressing in this recipe, laced with lemon and fresh dill makes the salad a favourite at this popular restaurant where it is served either warm or chilled.

3 tablespoons lemon juice, freshly squeezed

2–3 large garlic cloves, crushed

1 1/2 teaspoon Dijon mustard

1 teaspoon anchovy paste

1/2 teaspoon salt

1/2 teaspoon freshly ground black pepper

1/2 teaspoon sugar

1/4 cup vegetable oil

1/3 cup grated Parmesan cheese

5 cups small pasta shells

1/4 cup finely chopped fresh dill

3/4 pound small cooked shrimp

In a medium-sized bowl, stir together the lemon juice, garlic, Dijon mustard, anchovy paste, salt, pepper and sugar. Gradually whisk in the oil, then the Parmesan cheese and set aside.

Prepare pasta, drain and place in a large bowl. Pour dressing over pasta, tossing to coat. Stir in dill and shrimp. Serve either warm or chilled. Serves 6–8.

SEAFOOD PASTA SALAD

BILLY'S SEAFOOD COMPANY,
SAINT JOHN, NB

Chef Jason Cashin does not have to go very far from his kitchen to get the freshest of scallops and shrimps for this salad—the restaurant in Saint John's City Market is part of a fish market and oyster bar!

3 cups rotini pasta

2 tablespoons Dijon mustard

4 tablespoons egg-based mayonnaise

2 tablespoons liquid honey

1/4 pound cooked small scallops (80–100 count)

1/4 pound cooked salad shrimp (110–130 count)

kale leaves, as garnish

parsley sprigs, as garnish

In a large saucepan of salted water, cook pasta until *al dente*. Drain, rinse with cold water and thoroughly drain again.

In a small bowl, whisk together mustard, mayonnaise, and honey.

Place scallops and shrimp in bowl with pasta, drizzle with mayonnaise mixture and toss to coat.

Serve garnished with kale and parsley sprigs.

Serves 4.

Chef Jason Cashin's Seafood Pasta Salad ▶

AMHERST SHORE INN'S PASTA SALAD

AMHERST SHORE COUNTRY INN, LORNEVILLE, NS

Donna Laceby of the Amherst Shore Country Inn suggests preparing this dish early in the day, to allow time for the flavours to blend and the salad to chill.

1/2 cup olive oil

1/4 cup cider vinegar

2 tablespoons liquid honey

3 cloves garlic, finely minced

1/4 cup fresh herbs, chopped (basil, thyme, rosemary or marjoram)

1/4 cup fresh parsley, chopped

2 tablespoons tomato paste

1/2 teaspoon Worcestershire sauce

generous dash Tabasco sauce

1/3 cup water

salt and pepper, to taste

6 cups fresh tortellini

1 each bell peppers, red, green and yellow, in large julienne

1/2 cup chopped scallions

Using a wire whisk, combine oil, vinegar, honey, and garlic until emulsified. Stir in chopped herbs.

In a separate bowl whisk together the tomato paste, water, Worcestershire sauce, and Tabasco. Stir into oil mixture, season with salt and pepper and refrigerate.

Cook tortellini in boiling water. Drain and let cool.

In a large bowl, toss together the tortellini, peppers and scallions. Drizzle with dressing and stir well to coat. Refrigerate.

Serves 6.

Fresh herbs and colourful peppers accent the Amherst Shore Inn's Pasta Salad ▶

SEAFOOD

$\mathcal{F}$resh Atlantic seafood is an excellent choice for pasta dishes. In this section you will find a variety of recipes using the bounty of the sea.

◄ *Marshlands Inn's Fusilli with Jumbo Shrimp*

FUSILLI WITH JUMBO SHRIMP IN A PEPPERCORN CREAM SAUCE

MARSHLANDS INN, SACKVILLE, NB

A popular entrée at Marshlands Inn, chef Jeffrey Ayres serves this basil infused sauce with jumbo tiger shrimp and a colourful julienne of bell peppers.

1 pound black tiger shrimp (21–25 count)

2 cups heavy cream (35% m.f.)

2 cups milk (2% m.f.)

2–3 tablespoons dried basil, or to taste

1/4 cup white wine

2 tablespoons olive oil

1 red bell pepper, julienne

1 green bell pepper, julienne

1 red onion, peeled and thinly sliced

1 tablespoon green peppercorns in brine

1/2 cup brandy

tri-colour fusilli noodles to serve 4, cooked *al dente*

salt and pepper, to taste

Clean and devein shrimp, set aside.

In a heavy-bottomed saucepan, bring cream, milk, basil, and wine to a boil, reduce heat and simmer, stirring frequently, until sauce has thickened, approximately 30 minutes. Keep warm.

In a large skillet, heat olive oil and sauté shrimp 1 minute, add red and green peppers and onion and sauté 3 minutes, stirring frequently. Add green peppercorns and brandy and reduce. Stir in cream sauce and toss with hot pasta. Season with salt and pepper.

Serves 4.

SEAFOOD MEDLEY WITH CRAB ALFREDO SAUCE

BILLY'S SEAFOOD COMPANY, SAINT JOHN, NB

Tucked in the city market in downtown Saint John, the chef at Billy's Seafood Company provides the freshest of seafood entrées, using ingredients from their adjacent fish market.

3/4 pound shrimp (26–30 count)

1/2 pound scallops

1/2 pound lobster meat

1 cup mushrooms, sliced

1 cup mixed yellow, red and green peppers, julienne

1 tablespoon chopped garlic

1/2 cup white wine

1 cup water

spinach linguine, to serve six, cooked *al dente*

Crab Alfredo Sauce, recipe follows

Combine shrimp, scallops, lobster, mushrooms, peppers, garlic, wine and water in a covered skillet and bring to a boil. Immediately remove from heat and let stand 1 minute. Strain and keep warm.

Divide prepared linguine between four serving plates. Divide seafood and vegetables between plates and top with Crab Alfredo Sauce.

Serves 6.

Crab Alfredo Sauce

2 tablespoons butter

2 tablespoons chopped garlic

1/2 teaspoon cracked black pepper

1/2 cup white wine

2 cups cereal cream, blend or whole milk

5 tablespoons flour

1 cup shredded Parmesan cheese

7 ounces shredded crab meat

Melt butter in a large saucepan over medium heat. Add garlic, pepper and wine and cook 1 minute. Whisk in cream and sprinkle with flour. Bring to a boil, stirring constantly and cook until thickened. Stir in Parmesan cheese and crab meat, return to serving temperature.

Yields 3 1/2 cups sauce.

SEAFOOD LASAGNE

This "house speciality" was shared by a New Brunswick chef many years ago. The inn was perched on the Bay of Fundy shore, and the chef made use of the fresh seafood that was readily available.

1 1/2 pounds seafood (lobster, scallops, salmon or white fish in combination)

In boiling salted water, poach raw seafood until barely cooked. Drain and reserve.

1 pound spinach, rinsed and trimmed

Briefly cook spinach, drain well and chop.

4 eggs, lightly beaten

In a large bowl combine eggs, spinach, cottage cheese, nutmeg and season with salt and pepper. Set aside.

1 pound cottage cheese

1/8 teaspoon ground nutmeg

salt and pepper, to taste

6 tablespoons butter

1 medium onion, chopped

1 garlic clove, crushed

Melt butter and sauté onion and garlic until softened, being careful not to brown. Add dill, sprinkle with flour and bring to a simmer over medium heat, stirring constantly for 1 minute. Whisk sherry and cream, a little at a time, into flour mixture and cook until well blended and slightly thickened. Stir in Swiss cheese and reserved seafood and bring to serving temperature. Season with salt and pepper.

1 tablespoon fresh dill weed (1 teaspoon dried)

6 tablespoons flour

Preheat oven to 350°F.

salt and pepper, to taste

2 tablespoons sherry

3 cups light cream (10% m.f.)

1 cup grated Swiss cheese

To assemble, place half the prepared noodles in a greased 9 x 13-inch lasagne pan. Spread half the spinach mixture over the noodles and cover with half the seafood mixture. Repeat these 3 layers. Sprinkle top with Parmesan cheese and bake 45 minutes to 1 hour or until bubbly and browned. Remove from oven and let stand 10 minutes before serving.

10 lasagne noodles, cooked *al dente*

Serves 6–8.

1/2 cup grated Parmesan cheese

FETTUCCINI ALLA MARINERA

*First shared by Lunenburg innkeepers, this hearty rendition of classic tomato-based
marinara sauce features fresh Atlantic mussels, making it a substantial dish.*

1/4 cup olive oil

2 cloves garlic, minced

1 cup celery, thinly sliced

3/4 cup dry red wine

28-ounce can Italian-style tomatoes, chopped

28-ounce can tomato sauce

2 teaspoons dried oregano

2 teaspoons dried thyme

2 teaspoons fennel seeds

2 teaspoons dried parsley

1/4 teaspoon cayenne pepper

6 pounds fresh mussels, scrubbed and
debearded

1 cup water

1 teaspoon salt

fettuccini to serve 6–8, cooked *al dente*

freshly grated Parmesan cheese, as garnish

In a large, heavy-bottomed saucepan, heat oil
and sauté garlic and celery until tender. Stir in
wine, tomatoes, tomato sauce, oregano,
thyme, fennel, parsley and cayenne. Bring to a
boil, lower heat and simmer, stirring
occasionally, for 30 minutes.

Scrub and debeard mussels, discarding any
that are cracked or do not close when tapped.
Bring water and salt to a boil, add mussels and
steam 6 minutes or until mussels open. Shell
mussels, discarding any that do not open,
rinse and drain well. Add to tomato sauce.

While sauce is cooking, prepare fettuccini.
Serve sauce over fettuccini and garnished with
freshly grated Parmesan cheese.

Serves 6–8.

SPICY GARLIC SHRIMP LINGUINE

CHARLOTTE LANE CAFÉ AND
CRAFTS, SHELBURNE, NS

*Roland Glauser of the Charlotte Lane cautions
that this dish is a little bit hot but a whole lot
wonderful. I suggest adjusting the blackening spice
to suit your palate.*

2 tablespoons vegetable oil

1 pound large raw shrimp, peeled and
deveined (24–28 count)

1 tablespoon Cajun blackening spice, or to
taste

3 cloves garlic, minced

1 cup heavy cream (35% m.f.)

4 cups puréed tomato sauce

linguine to serve 4, cooked *al dente*

Heat oil in a large skillet and sauté shrimp,
blackening spice and garlic for 30 seconds. Add
cream and tomato sauce, reduce heat and
simmer until shrimp are cooked, approximately
3 minutes.

Serve over linguine.

Serves 4.

Spicy Garlic Shrimp Linguine as served at the Charlotte Lane Café ▶

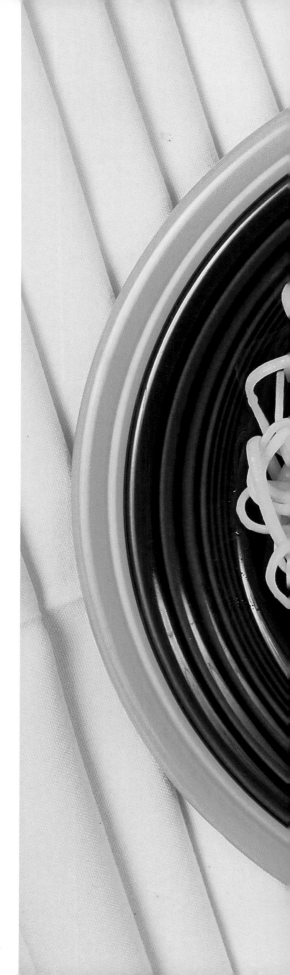

FETTUCCINI WITH LOBSTER AND TARRAGON

BLOMIDON INN, WOLFVILLE, NS

Innkeeper Donna Laceby of Wolfville's famed Blomidon Inn advises that this is one of her most sought-after recipes. We are fortunate that she is willing to share her culinary riches.

1 cup onions, finely chopped

4 tablespoon olive oil

2 cups plum tomatoes, peeled, seeded and chopped

2–3 teaspoons tarragon

salt and pepper, to taste

2 cups heavy cream (35% m.f.)

Pinch cayenne pepper

1 1/2 pounds lobster meat

fettuccini or other fine pasta to serve 4, cooked *al dente*

fresh parsley and tarragon, as garnish

Sweat onions in oil for 20 minutes, being careful not to brown. Add tomatoes and tarragon. Bring to a boil and season with salt and pepper. Reduce heat and simmer, covered, for 30 minutes. Let cool and purée in a food processor.

Return tomato mixture to a saucepan and add cream. Bring to a simmer and reduce slightly. Stir in cayenne and lobster, return to serving temperature and serve over pasta of choice. Garnish with fresh parsley and fresh tarragon.

Serves 4.

Blomidon Inn's famous Fettuccini with Lobster and Tarragon ▶

PASTA ATLANTIC

FALCOURT INN, NICTAUX, NS

Fresh Atlantic seafood and pasta — a marriage made in heaven!

1 pound mussels, scrubbed and steamed

1/4 cup garlic butter, see page 44

1/2 cup grated Parmesan cheese

1 tablespoon vegetable oil

1/3 pound each haddock fillet, skinless salmon and scallops in bite-sized pieces

1/4 cup flour

1/2 pound jumbo shrimp (11–15 count)

salt and pepper, to taste

linguine to serve 4, cooked *al dente*

Pasta Atlantic Seafood Sauce, recipe follows

assorted steamed vegetables, as garnish

Steam mussels in a little water until open, about 7 minutes. Drain, discard any mussels that do not open. Keep warm

In a small saucepan, over medium heat, melt garlic butter and stir in Parmesan cheese. Stir to combine then set aside and keep warm.

Heat oil in a large skillet over medium-high. Dust haddock, scallops, and salmon with flour and sauté. Turn fish and add shrimps and cook 1 minute. Turn shrimp and pour in garlic butter mixture, cover pan shake, then remove from heat. Season with salt and pepper.

To serve, divide pasta between four shallow bowls. Arrange mussels around outside edge, top with remaining seafood and drizzle with Pasta Atlantic Seafood Sauce. Garnish with steamed vegetables.

Serves 4.

Pasta Atlantic Seafood Sauce

4 tablespoons each butter and flour

2 cups chicken broth

1/2 cup sliced mushrooms

2 garlic cloves, crushed

1/3 cup each sweet sherry and heavy cream

Melt butter over medium heat and whisk in flour. Cook roux, stirring constantly for 2 minutes. Whisk in broth, bring to a boil, reduce heat and simmer until thickened. Set aside. In a saucepan simmer mushrooms and garlic in sherry until barely tender. Stir in cream, cook 4 minutes, stirring often. Combine with sauce and bring to serving temperature.

Chef Kelvin Boutilier of Falcourt Inn's Pasta Atlantic ▶

THE LEDGES PASTA WITH SHRIMP

THE LEDGES INN, DOAKTOWN, NB

This is a delightful pasta dish, readily made with ingredients in the pantry and freezer.

1 medium onion, diced

2 cloves garlic, minced

1 teaspoon fresh sage (1/4 teaspoon dried)

1 tablespoon olive oil

1 cup tomato sauce

1/3 cup red wine

1 tablespoon butter

1 tablespoon freshly squeezed lemon juice

2 tablespoons brandy

dried chili flakes, optional, to taste

3–4 drops Tabasco sauce

24 large raw shrimp, peeled and deveined

flour for dredging

2 tablespoons olive oil

Lemon pepper linguine, to serve 4, cooked *al dente*

In a large skillet, sauté onion, garlic, and sage in hot oil until tender, approximately 2–3 minutes. Stir in tomato sauce, wine, butter, lemon juice, brandy, chili flakes, and Tabasco sauce. Simmer 3–4 minutes, set aside and keep warm.

While sauce is cooking dredge shrimp in flour and quickly pan fry in olive oil tossing frequently until done, about 4 minutes. Shrimp will turn pink and become firm. Do not overcook.

To serve, divide linguine between 4 serving plates. Top with shrimp and drizzle with sauce.

Serves 4.

GABRIEAU'S FETTUCCINI WITH SCALLOPS AND SHRIMP

GABRIEAU'S BISTRO, ANTIGONISH, NS

*Created by owner-chef Mark Gabrieau, this entrée is easy to prepare
and sure to become a family favourite.*

1 1/2 tablespoons olive oil

1 1/2 tablespoons butter

3/4 pound bay scallops (90–100 count)

3/4 pound medium shrimp, cooked, peeled
and deveined (30–35 count)

1 red pepper, roasted and sliced*

1 cup peas

1 large garlic clove, minced

1 tablespoon chopped fresh tarragon (1
teaspoon dried)

salt and pepper, to taste

1/2 cup white wine

1 cup heavy cream (35% m.f.)

fettuccini to serve 4, cooked *al dente*

fresh parsley, chopped, as garnish

freshly grated Parmesan cheese, as garnish

Heat olive oil and butter over medium-high heat in a large skillet. Add scallops, shrimp, red peppers, peas, garlic, and tarragon and sauté 2–3 minutes. Season with salt and pepper. Remove to a plate and keep warm.

Deglaze pan with white wine, stir in cream and bring to a boil. Reduce heat and simmer until slightly thickened. Add fettuccini and toss to coat. Stir in reserved vegetables and serve garnished with fresh parsley and grated Parmesan cheese.

Serves 4.

* To roast a red pepper: Grill pepper until it is burnt black on all sides. Immediately place in a brown paper bag until cooled. Peel blacked skin from pepper. Remove stalk and inner seeds and slice.

THE DUNES' THAI SHRIMP LINGUINE

THE DUNES, BRACKLEY BEACH, PEI

Chef Shaun McKay of the Dunes cautions that this is a fairly hot dish and that the Thai Peanut Sauce may be moderated by using less crushed chilis. You be the judge!

2–3 tablespoons sesame oil

4 green onions

1 large red bell pepper, julienne

4 plum tomatoes, diced

2 cloves garlic, minced

24 raw jumbo shrimp, deveined and shelled (11–15 count)

linguine to serve 4, cooked *al dente*

Thai Peanut Sauce, recipe follows

In a large skillet heat oil over medium-high and sauté onions, peppers, tomatoes and garlic for 2 minutes, stirring frequently. Add shrimp and toss in pan for 2–3 minutes, being careful not to overcook. Add Thai Peanut Sauce, return to serving temperature and toss with cooked pasta.

Serves 4.

Thai Peanut Sauce

2 garlic cloves, minced

1/4 cup soy sauce

2/3 cup creamy peanut butter

1 tablespoon brown sugar

1 1/3 cups water

2 tablespoons fresh ginger, minced

1 teaspoon crushed chilis, or to taste

In a saucepan bring all ingredients to a boil. Reduce heat and simmer 5 minutes, stirring constantly.

The Dunes' Thai Shrimp Linguine beautifully presented by Chef Shaun McKay ▶

P.E.I. MUSSELS WITH ANGEL HAIR PASTA

CATHERINE MCKINNON'S SPOT O'TEA RESTAURANT, STANLEY BRIDGE, PEI

Angel hair or capelli d'angelo pasta is a delicate noodle, usually served with a light sauce. At the Spot O'Tea Restaurant, chef Harry Pineau serves pasta with warm baguette slices and a green salad.

2 pounds fresh mussels

3 tablespoons garlic butter*

2 tablespoons flour

1 1/4 cups reserved mussel broth

1/2 cup dry white wine

1–2 tablespoons chopped parsley

salt and freshly ground pepper, to taste

angel hair pasta to serve 4, cooked *al dente*

Scrub mussels and debeard, discarding any that do not close when tapped and rinsed under cold water. In a large kettle bring a cup or so of water to a boil, add mussels and steam until mussels open, approximately 6 minutes. Discard any mussels that do not open. Strain mussel liquid and reserve. Remove mussels from shells and set aside.

Melt butter in a large saucepan and whisk in flour. Cook roux stirring constantly 2 minutes, being careful not to brown. Whisk in reserved mussel broth and wine and continue cooking until sauce has thickened. Stir in reserved mussels and parsley. Season with salt and freshly ground pepper. Combine prepared pasta and sauce and serve in heated bowls.

Serves 4.

* Garlic Butter

Stir 2–3 minced cloves of garlic into 1/2 cup softened butter. Store refrigerated in a covered container.

Spot O'Tea's P.E.I. Mussels with Angel Hair Pasta ▶

FRESH SEAFOOD LINGUINE WITH THAI RED CURRY SAUCE

ARBOR VIEW INN, LUNENBURG, NS

Owner-chef Daniel Orovec advises that coconut milk, red curry paste, lime leaves, and Asian fish sauce are available at Asian grocery markets or well stocked grocery stores. The Red Curry Sauce offers a complexity of flavours which combine beautifully with fresh seafood.

1 1/2 pounds mixed fresh seafood (scallops, raw shrimp, mussels or salmon chunks)

Red Curry Sauce, recipe follows

linguine to serve 4, cooked *al dente*

fresh cilantro, chopped as garnish

Rinse scallops and, if large, cut in half.

Shell and devein shrimp and cut skinless and boneless salmon fillet into bite-sized pieces.

Scrub mussels and debeard. Steam mussels in a little water until opened, approximately 6 minutes. Remove from heat, discard any that do not open, shuck and keep warm.

Prepare Red Curry Sauce and add uncooked seafood. Cover and simmer until fish is cooked, approximately 4 minutes. Stir in cooked mussels.

Add sauce to cooked linguine and toss to coat. Serve in pasta bowls with a sprinkling of fresh cilantro.

Serves 4.

Red Curry Sauce

1 1/2 tablespoons red curry paste

1 teaspoon palm sugar or brown sugar

3 1/2 cups coconut milk

Asian fish sauce, to taste

3 Kaffir Lime Leaves, crumbled or 1 stalk fresh lemon grass* (minced)

In a saucepan, over medium heat, gently warm curry paste and sugar until fragrant. Stir in coconut milk and add remaining ingredients. Bring to a boil, reduce heat and simmer 15 minutes to allow flavours to blend. Strain sauce and adjust seasonings to taste.

* Fresh lemon grass stalks range from pale to medium green with a whitish bulb. Gently bruise the stalk for optimum flavour, then peel away the outer layer and mince.

Arbor View Inn's Fresh Seafood Linguine with Thai Red Curry Sauce ▶

CONCHIGLIONI WITH SMOKED SALMON AND RICOTTA FILLING

THE WINDSOR HOUSE OF ST. ANDREWS, ST. ANDREWS, NB

Chef Patricia Bullock fills her shell-shaped conchiglioni pasta with mild ricotta cheese and distinctly flavoured smoked salmon. The dish may be prepared in advance and refrigerated until baking time, thus making it an ideal entrée for entertaining.

30 jumbo conchiglioni

Filling

16 ounces ricotta cheese

5 ounces smoked salmon, diced

2 teaspoons chopped fresh dill

2 teaspoons chopped chives

1 cup freshly grated Parmesan cheese

1 teaspoon freshly grated black pepper

1 tablespoon chopped dill or chives, as garnish

Sauce

1/4 cup butter

1/2 cup flour

2 cups white wine or champagne

1 bay leaf

2 teaspoons salt

pinch cayenne pepper

2 cups milk

1 cup heavy cream (35% m.f.)

Bring a large pot of salted water to a boil. Cook pasta until *al dente* then transfer to a bowl of ice water to stop the cooking process. Remove from water and turn shells upside down to drain.

Combine all the filling ingredients in a bowl and set aside.

In a medium saucepan melt butter and whisk in flour. Cook over medium heat for two minutes, stirring constantly. Whisk in wine and cook until mixture is smooth. Add bay leaf, salt, and cayenne. As mixture begins to thicken, whisk in milk and cream, 1/2 cup at a time. Cook over low heat for 20 minutes. Remove bay leaf, and keep warm.

Preheat oven to 350°F.

Spread a 3/4-inch layer of sauce over the bottom of a large oven proof baking dish. Reserve remaining sauce and keep warm.

Fill shells with a rounded tablespoon of filling and place them in the dish close enough together so that they do not fall over. Bake, covered for 15 minutes. Remove cover and bake an additional 5 minutes until the filling is slightly browned.

Serve on a bed of warm sauce, garnished with chopped dill or chives.

Serves 6–8.

Conchiglioni with Smoked Salmon and Ricotta as served in the dining room at the ▶ Windsor House of St. Andrews

ENTRÉES

The secret to these recipes is using the freshest of available ingredients. Full-flavoured vegetables, freshly grated cheese, plus a pungent sauce brings instant success!

◀ *Penne Chicken Pollo, the creation of chef Mark Gabrieau of Gabrieau's Bistro*

PENNE CHICKEN POLLO WITH WILD MUSHROOMS IN PORT CREAM SAUCE

GABRIEAU'S BISTRO, ANTIGONISH, NS

Chef Mark Gabrieau is master of his own kitchen at his bistro.
It is a special treat to have this recipe.

2-3 tablespoons olive oil

l large leek, diced (white part only)

1 small onion, diced

8 ounces wild mushrooms, sliced

8 ounces button mushrooms, sliced

1 clove garlic, minced

1 pound chicken breast, boneless and skinless, thinly sliced

salt and pepper, to taste

2 teaspoon Pommery mustard*

1/2 tablespoon pesto

1/2 tablespoon butter

1/2 cup port

1/2 cup heavy cream (35% m.f.)

penne pasta to serve 4, cooked *al dente*

cracked pepper, as garnish

chopped parsley, as garnish

parmesan cheese, as garnish

Heat olive oil in a large skillet over medium-high heat and sauté leeks, onions, mushrooms, garlic, and chicken, season with salt and pepper. Stir in mustard, pesto, and butter and continue to cook only until chicken is no longer pink in the centre. Remove to a plate and keep warm.

Deglaze pan with port, stirring up any brown bits that might be in the bottom of the pan. Add the cream, bring to a boil then reduce heat and simmer until sauce has thickened. Stir in reserved vegetables and chicken. Add pasta, tossing to coat. Garnish with a generous amount of cracked pepper, chopped parsley, and Parmesan cheese.

Serves 4.

* Pommery mustard is a French-style mustard with seeds.

SPICY PASTA WITH CHEESE

THE WHITMAN INN, KEMPT, NS

*Served with a salad and crusty bread, this hearty pasta dish will satisfy
the most discerning palate.*

4 tablespoons butter

2 medium onions, chopped

3 cloves garlic, mashed

4 tablespoons flour

1 tablespoon pickled banana pepper or jalapeno pepper, minced

1 1/2 teaspoons ground coriander

2 teaspoons ground cumin

3 1/2 cups diced stewed tomatoes

6 ounces cream cheese, softened and in small cubes

1/2 cup grated Monterey Jack cheese

1 cup grated Parmesan cheese

1 cup grated cheddar cheese

1 pound fusilli, cooked *al dente*

1 cup fresh bread cubes

1/4 cup butter, melted

Preheat oven to 350°F.

In a large saucepan, melt butter and sauté onion and garlic until softened. Sprinkle with flour and stir in peppers, coriander, cumin and stewed tomatoes. Simmer 3 minutes until slightly thickened and stir in cheeses and cooked pasta. Turn into an oven-proof baking dish.

Toss bread cubes with melted butter and place on top of casserole. Bake until bubbly and slightly browned.

Serves 6.

THAI CHICKEN PENNE

DUNDEE ARMS INN, CHARLOTTETOWN, PEI

Chef Austin Clements of the Dundee Arms prepares his penne pasta dish with colourful crisp vegetables and sesame-infused chicken pieces. For those who like a spicier dish, he serves the pasta accompanied by a small amount of chili sauce on the side.

penne pasta to serve 4, cooked *al dente*

4 teaspoons sesame oil

1 pound boneless and skinless chicken breast, in thin strips

1 can baby corn, 14-ounce size

1/2 each red, yellow and green pepper, cut julienne

2 carrots, peeled and cut julienne

4 green onions, sliced

1 small head broccoli, cut into small flowerettes

1/4 cup hoisin sauce

4 tablespoons chili sauce

1/4 cup honey

1/4 cup hummus

3 tablespoons sesame seeds

salt and pepper, to taste

additional chili sauce, if desired

Prepare pasta, drain, rinse and set aside.

In a large saucepan heat sesame oil and sauté chicken strips for 2 minutes. Add corn, peppers, carrots, onions, and broccoli and cook, stirring frequently until vegetables are crisp tender, approximately 3 minutes. Add hoisin sauce, chili sauce and honey and toss until well coated. Stir in hummus and sesame seeds, cook 1–2 minutes, then toss with pasta. Season with salt and pepper and serve with additional chili sauce on the side.

Serves 4.

Thai Chicken Penne from the dining room of the Dundee Arms ▶

THREE-CHEESE PASTA PRIMAVERA

BLOMIDON INN, WOLFVILLE, NS

Fresh vegetables, in season, plus a careful blend of grated Parmesan, Cheddar and Swiss cheeses makes chef Keith Bond's pasta dish a filling meal for two.

1 1/2 cups fresh vegetables

1/4 cup white wine

1 teaspoon vegetable stock

3/4 cup heavy cream (35% m.f.)

1 cup penne pasta, cooked *al dente*

1/2 cup mixed grated cheese, Parmesan, Cheddar and Swiss

salt and freshly grated black pepper, to taste

Prepare vegetables in small bite-sized pieces. In a saucepan, blanch vegetables in boiling water for approximately 2 minutes. Drain, reserving 1 teaspoon water. Rinse with cold water to stop cooking process and set aside.

In a medium saucepan reduce wine by one half. Stir in cream and reserved stock, bring to a boil and reduce by one half.

To serve, toss cooked pasta with vegetables and cream sauce. Immediately stir in cheeses and season with salt and grated black pepper.

Serves 2

SICILIAN PASTA

MARSHLANDS INN, SACKVILLE, NB

Crisp vegetables served in a light sauce make this an excellent vegetarian entrée, or if served in smaller portions, an innovative appetizer.

1/2 cup olive oil

4 medium tomatoes, in 1-inch dice

8 ounces fresh mushrooms, sliced

1 medium red onion, peeled and in 1-inch dice

4–6 cloves garlic, puréed

1/4 pound snow peas, trimmed and sliced

3–4 tablespoons chopped fresh basil

salt and pepper, to taste

3 cups chicken stock or water

2/3 cup grated Parmesan cheese, divided

spinach fettuccini to serve 4, cooked *al dente*

fresh basil leaves, as garnish

Heat olive oil in a large skillet over high heat and sauté tomatoes, mushrooms, onion, garlic, snow peas, and basil for 2 minutes. Season with salt and pepper. Add stock or water and 1/3 cup of the Parmesan cheese. Bring to a boil and toss with cooked pasta.

Serve garnished with remaining cheese and basil.

Serves 4.

JACK'S GLORIOUS GOULASH

THE INNLET CAFÉ, MAHONE BAY, NS

Owner-chef Jack Sorenson perfected this recipe many years ago. If tamari sauce is unavailable, substitute soya sauce. The recipe is, indeed, glorious!

1 1/2 pounds cubed beef steak

1 medium onion, sliced

2 garlic cloves, crushed

1 cup stewed tomatoes, chopped

1 tablespoon cider vinegar

2 cups water

1 teaspoon paprika

1 tablespoon tamari sauce

1/2 teaspoon salt

1/4 teaspoon pepper

1/2 teaspoon caraway seeds, crushed

1/4 teaspoon marjoram

2 tablespoons flour

2 cups mushrooms, sliced

egg noodles to serve 4, cooked *al dente*

Place beef, onion, garlic, tomatoes, vinegar, water, paprika and tamari in a large saucepan and bring to a simmer. Add salt, pepper, caraway, and marjoram and simmer 1 1/2 hours, until meat is fork-tender.

Remove meat from saucepan and measure volume of liquid. Bring to 1 1/3 cups by reducing or adding water. Mix flour with enough water to make a paste, combine with a bit of the cooking liquid and stir into sauce. Simmer, stirring until thickened. Add mushrooms and simmer 5 minutes. Return meat to the sauce and bring to serving temperature. Serve over cooked noodles.

Serves 6.

FETTUCCINI AND CREAM

THE MURRAY MANOR BED AND
BREAKFAST, YARMOUTH, NS

*Served with warm bread and a tossed salad, this
delightful pasta dish is a filling vegetarian entrée.
Innkeeper Joan Semple admits she has doubled the
recipe with success, making it an easy-to-prepare
dish suitable for eight servings.*

8 ounces fettuccini

1/2 cup unsalted butter, melted

1 cup heavy cream, (35% m.f.)

3/4 cup Parmesan cheese

generous dash of nutmeg

salt and pepper, to taste

Cook fettuccini in boiling, salted water until
al dente. Drain and keep warm. In a saucepan,
over medium heat, melt butter, whisk in
cream and Parmesan cheese. Season sauce
with nutmeg, salt and pepper. Gently toss into
warm pasta.

Serves 4.

SPAGHETTINI GORGONZOLA

CHARLOTTE LANE CAFÉ AND
CRAFTS, SHELBURNE, NS

*Infused with the flavour of Gorgonzola cheese, this
easy pasta dish is served by owner-chef Roland
Glauser garnished with sprigs of fresh rosemary.*

2 tablespoons vegetable oil

1 1/4 pounds chicken breasts, boneless and
skinless, thinly sliced

3 cloves garlic, finely chopped

1 small bunch fresh broccoli, in florets

2 cups heavy cream (35% m.f.)

1 tablespoon green peppercorns

12 ounces Gorgonzola cheese, crumbled

1/4 teaspoon curry

salt and pepper, to taste

spaghettini to serve 4, cooked *al dente*

paprika, as garnish

fresh rosemary sprigs, as garnish

Heat oil in a large skillet over medium high
heat. Quickly stir-fry chicken and garlic for 1
minute. Add broccoli and stir fry an additional
minute. Stir in cream, peppercorns, cheese,
and curry. Reduce heat and simmer until
chicken is cooked and broccoli is crisp.

Serve over pasta garnished with a sprinkling
of paprika and fresh rosemary sprigs.

Serves 4.

VERMICELLI WITH MUSHROOM CREAM SAUCE

This simple to prepare recipe was shared by a Nova Scotia innkeeper some years ago. If possible, use a variety of mushrooms such as portobello, shiitake and button. Serve a small portion as an appetizer or, combined with a salad and crusty bread, the dish becomes delicious vegetarian fare.

1/2 cup scallions, chopped

3/4 cup butter

3 cups mushrooms, sliced

5 tablespoons flour

2 cups milk

1 1/2 cups mozzarella cheese, grated

1/2 cup grated Parmesan cheese

salt and pepper, to taste

vermicelli or other pasta to serve 4, cooked *al dente*

fresh parsley, as garnish

Sauté scallions in butter over medium heat for several minutes. Add mushrooms and sauté an additional 5 to 10 minutes, stirring frequently.

Sprinkle with flour and stir in milk, a little at a time, and cook until sauce is smooth and slightly thickened. Add cheeses and stir. Season with salt and pepper. Serve over hot vermicelli or pasta of choice, garnish with fresh parsley.

Serves 4.

TORTELLINI WITH ROASTED RED PEPPERS AND SPINACH

THE DUNES CAFÉ, BRACKLEY BEACH, PEI

Chef Shaun McKay serves this rich spinach and pepper dish as either an appetizer or vegetarian main course.

1 clove garlic, minced

1 tablespoons olive oil

2 cups heavy cream (35% m.f.)

4 ounces Gorgonzola cheese, crumbled

6 ounces fresh spinach, rinsed, dried and stems removed

1 red pepper, roasted and julienned*

1/2 pound package cheese tortellini, cooked *al dente*

salt and pepper, to taste

In a medium-sized saucepan sweat garlic in olive oil for 1 minute, being careful not to brown. Stir in cream and simmer until sauce begins to thicken. Add cheese and stir until blended. Stir in spinach and mix until leaves begin to wilt. Add roasted pepper and cooked pasta. Season with salt and pepper. Serves 4 as an appetizer or 2 as a main course.

* To roast a red pepper: Grill pepper until it is burnt black on all sides. Immediately place in a brown paper bag until cooled. Peel blackened skin from pepper, remove stalk and inner seeds and slice.

SEASONS IN THYME'S CHICKEN AND ASPARAGUS FETTUCCINI

SEASONS IN THYME, SUMMERSIDE, PEI

Owner-chef Stefan Czapalay presents a pleasant combination in his asparagus and chicken pasta dish. The sauce, with the addition of sherry, cumin, and coriander has a unique flavour, yet the dish is simple for the home cook to prepare.

fettuccini to serve 4

3 tablespoons olive oil

1/4 pound fresh asparagus

3 tablespoons butter, divided

1 pound chicken breast, boneless and skinless, diced

1 shallot, finely diced

1 garlic clove, minced

1/2 teaspoon cumin

1/2 teaspoon coriander

pinch turmeric

1/2 teaspoon salt

1/2 teaspoon freshly ground pepper

1/3 cup white wine

2 tablespoons sherry

1/3 cup chicken stock

1/2 cup heavy cream (35% m.f.)

In a large pot of boiling, salted water, cook fettuccini until just tender. Drain, rinse, and drain again. Place noodles in a warm bowl, drizzle with olive oil, gently toss to coat, and keep warm.

In a medium saucepan, blanch asparagus in boiling water until just tender, approximately 1–2 minutes. Drain, dot with 1 teaspoon of the butter and keep warm.

In a non-stick skillet, melt 1 tablespoon butter over medium high heat. Add chicken and cook until all the pieces have browned slightly. Add shallots and garlic, sauté until translucent. Sprinkle with cumin, coriander, turmeric, salt and pepper and stir until chicken is evenly coated. Add wine, sherry, and stock and continue cooking until liquid has reduced its volume by half. Stir in cream and remaining butter. Continue cooking until slightly thickened, add asparagus and toss to coat. Serve on a bed of fettuccini.

Serves 4.

Chicken and Asparagus Fettuccini as presented tableside at Seasons in Thyme Restaurant ▶

CHARLOTTE LANE'S LINGUINE SIAM

CHARLOTTE LANE CAFÉ AND CRAFTS, SHELBURNE, NS

Chef Roland Glauser suggests any combination of fresh vegetables works well in this dish. At the Charlotte Lane, he combines broccoli with cauliflower, mushrooms, tomato wedges, water chestnuts, fresh beans and snow peas. If you enjoy fresh vegetables, you will love the marriage of the pickled ginger and hoisin sauce as presented in this dish.

2 tablespoons sesame oil

2 cloves garlic, finely chopped

3 cups fresh vegetables, in bite-sized pieces

2/3 cup water

1 1/2 tablespoons chopped pickled ginger*

2/3 cup hoisin sauce

cornstarch, to thicken, optional

Linguine to serve 4, cooked *al dente*

Heat oil over medium high in a large skillet. Quickly stir fry garlic and vegetables for 1–2 minutes. Add water, cover and steam until vegetables are crisp tender. Stir in ginger and hoisin sauce and thicken with a little cornstarch, if desired. Toss with hot linguine.

Serves 4.

* Pickled ginger is sold by the jar in Asian markets and some larger grocery stores.

MURRAY MANOR PASTA WITH ARTICHOKE SAUCE

THE MURRAY MANOR BED AND BREAKFAST, YARMOUTH, NS

This recipe is the answer for the day when unexpected guests arrive and the larder is almost bare. Innkeeper Joan Semple whisks together this delightful sauce using ingredients she has on hand.

2 jars marinated artichokes, 6-ounce size

1 tablespoon butter

1 medium onion, diced

2 tablespoons fresh basil, diced (2 teaspoons dried)

1/2 cup sour cream

1/2 cup creamy cottage cheese

salt and pepper, to taste

linguine to serve 4

freshly grated Parmesan cheese, as garnish

fresh basil sprigs, as garnish

Drain artichokes and reserve marinade. Quarter artichokes and set aside.

In a medium-sized skillet, melt butter and sauté onion until softened being careful not to brown. Stir in artichokes, reserved marinade, basil, sour cream and cottage cheese. Season with salt and pepper and keep warm.

In a large saucepan, cook pasta until *al dente*. Drain and toss with warm sauce. Garnish dish with grated Parmesan and a sprig of fresh basil.

Serves 4.

SPOT O'TEA PASTA PRIMAVERA

CATHERINE MCKINNON'S SPOT O'TEA RESTAURANT, STANLEY BRIDGE, PEI

"Primavera" is the Italian word denoting fresh spring vegetables and, at the Spot O'Tea, chef Harry Pineau makes the fresh produce the features of his pasta dish!

2 cups chicken stock, homemade preferred

pinch each ground ginger, garlic powder, and thyme

2 teaspoons soy sauce

2 teaspoons white wine

salt and white pepper, to taste

1/4 cup butter

1/3 cup flour

1 cup milk

1/3 cup heavy cream (35% m.f.)

2–3 cups assorted vegetables diced into small cubes (cauliflower, broccoli, snow peas, carrots, red onion, red pepper, etc.)

fettuccini or linguine to serve 4, cooked *al dente*

freshly grated Parmesan cheese, as garnish

In a large saucepan bring stock to a boil and add ginger, garlic, thyme, soy sauce, wine, salt and pepper.

In a separate saucepan melt butter and whisk in flour. Cook roux for 2 minutes, stirring constantly and being careful not to brown it. Whisk chicken stock into roux and bring to a boil. Stir in milk and cream and return to a simmer until mixture thickens. Set aside and keep warm.

Trim vegetables to a uniform size and blanch or sauté until crisp tender. Stir into sauce.

To serve, divide cooked pasta between serving plates and top with primavera sauce. Garnish with freshly grated Parmesan cheese.

Serves 4.